Remote / WebCam Notarization

BASIC UNDERSTANDING

Jeannie Eunice Franks

Other books by the author:

Available at:
https://www.notarynow.club/buynow

Notary Public Essentials:

Helpful Knowledge for all Commissioned Notaries in the United States of America.

Commissioning as Notary Public & Notary Signing Agent at 40+.

From Military to Civilian:

Transitioning from War and Guns to Online Notarization Specialist.

FROM THE CYBER EDUCATION SERIES

Customer Service, Technology & Remote/Webcam Notarization:
Aiming for the Five Stars Every Time.

Cyber Aware:
The Code

Cyber Insurance Explained.

First Printing: 2018

ISBN 978-1-387-96407-9

Self Published. Year of our Lord 2018

PO Box 7170
Hampton, Virginia 23666
https://www.virginianotary.club

Ordering Information:

Special discounts are available on quantity purchases by corporations, associations, educators, and others. For details, contact the publisher at the above listed address or e-mail the publisher at myvirginianotary@gmail.com

U.S trade bookstores and wholesalers: please contact Jeannie Eunice Franks at myvirginianotary@gmail.com

About the Cover of the book: designed by Jeannie Eunice Franks.

The wet-inked notarial feather becomes inkless once it enters cyberspace. Tiny dots of light become the notarial ink that has the capacity to write the invisible language of ones and zeros. Jeannie E. Franks. 2018.

Dedication

To God.
Thank you for giving me the gift of grace and ability to persevere.

To my lovely husband Kansas.
Thank you. Without your support and patience, I would have never achieved my dream.

To my brother Roger.
Thank you for reminding me that it will happen if I get to it.
Me: "I want to write a book."
My brother: "Who or what is preventing you from writing it?"

To my family.
From the youngest to the oldest, including pets, everyone in my family has been a teacher in my life.

To seasoned and new commissioned Notaries.
Your conversations and application of the craft revealed a lot.
Thank you for your contribution in the past and during transitional times such as this; Electronic/Remote notarization.

Contents

Acknowledgements

I would like to thank Lulu.com, my mentors, my creative writing colleagues, and my family without whose help this book would have never been completed and distributed. Thank you for your patience and guidance.

I would also like to thank the Notary Associations that do their best to provide access to up-to-date notarial information, education, and other member's benefits. Moreover, I would like to thank the National Association of Secretary of States (NASS) for its continued effort to promote understanding on issues related to technologies that enables remote notarizations.

Preface

As more States in the United States of America accept and adapt to Remote/WebCam notarization, there is a basic understanding in the process that Notaries Public need and want to keep in mind: when we deal with online transactions, we participate in a cyberspace environment. That position places the Remote or WebCam Notaries in the frontline of our Nation's defense when countering Cyber-warfare. In a way, when notaries public provide Remote/WebCam notarization, that makes Cyber-Notaries fraud-deterrent agents in the cyber environment.

More than reviewing your State or Commonwealth Laws often, becoming familiarized with the proper maintenance of the hardware, software, and the recommended online companies that facilitate online signing are only a few good practices that should become natural habits for Cyber-Notaries.

This book is mostly intended to make Remote/WebCam Notaries, or what I call Cyber-Notaries, aware of the sensible side of the Cyber-environment. It is true that there is a lot of flexibility protected by encryption; however, the cyber-environment protection will still depend on cyber-notaries by following proper steps and by developing good habits when performing cyber-notarizations.

Introduction

It is in my understanding that Remote/WebCam notarization is still in its infancy, however, utilizing electronic equipment has been part of society in the United States of America for quite a while already. Many have adapted habits that are not healthy for the Cyber environment, protection of the Cyberspace, and the identity of signers. As a responsible public officer in charge of ensuring the signers are who they say they are, the same way notaries public guard the information of signers in traditional ways, now new notaries, commissioned as electronic notaries and providing remote/WebCam notarizations, must adapt to secured electronic measurements due to the openness of the internet.

Most likely, at some point, in the life of every resident in the United States of America, there will be the need of figuring out who will notarize that resident's documents. At every place anyone has been, a notarization has taken place or that place has been linked to a notarial act; from simple acknowledgement to notarizing a signature by mark. All these processes where the presence and official seal of a Notary are mandatory are now taking place in cyberspace where the presence of clever hackers should not be undermined. Hackers are becoming so common that even our Nation's defense developed a CyberCommand[1] dedicated to detect unsolicited cyber-intrusion and other cyber-related issues.

Remote/WebCam Notarization: Basic Understanding intends to navigate your thoughts through basic foundational development of a CyberNotary, the implications of being one, proper Remote/WebCam notarization, and teachable tips to help other notaries to gain the same knowledge and attitude when dealing with notarizations in a cyber-environment.

---

[1] USCYBERCOM. https://www.cybercom.mil

Chapter 1: Becoming a CyberNotary

As far as I am concerned, before a resident of the United States of America can apply to be commissioned as Electronic Notary , the person must be commissioned as a Traditional Notary first. Each State and Commonwealth of the United States has its own laws which each notary public must abide by. Always check the laws of the State or Commonwealth you are intending to become a Notary Public at.

One of the great things about being trained as a traditional notary public before becoming an electronic notary is the opportunity given to absorb the signature signing process, the ability to identify the true identity of the signer, recognize when there might be unwillingness to sign, and the implication of being an official public officer.

The responsibilities of a Notary Public dates back to 2750 BC[2] when the notary was also known as scribe, and was part of the bureaucracy. Back then, scribes, at least in Egypt, did not have to pay taxes, join the military, nor engage in manual labor. Today, notaries public, pay taxes, join the military if they want, and engage in manual labor if there is the need or desire for it. Other publications state that the Notary Public profession dates back to Roman Times. Whichever the case, the responsibility has always been of great importance even when it has been considered "behind the scenes." This is a job that, now-a-day, many people do, but no-one really knows about it unless the notary let others know. The hidden status of a Notary Public may start to shift to a more public face as well due to the increased use of social media. After all, a Notary Public is a Public Officer needed by many people to move on in certain transactions, and committed to the State to assist on keeping the system moving smoothly, and deterring fraud in the process.

---

[2] BC is used to label or number years in the Julian and Gregorian Calendars and it means "Before Christ"; years before the birth of Jesus of Nazareth.

The responsibility of a Notary Public may not be considered "Royal" in the United States of America today, but it helps to keep the wheels of a society moving forward. What a Notary Public does or omits on a document today is as good today as it will be in the future, or so I learned in my latest refresher Notary course. Recently, I learned that there has been court cases that had to look back 25 years of documentation in order to find the seal of a notary and the Notary's notes dated 25 years ago. No doubt, what a notary does today might be the key of a court case tomorrow.

Becoming a CyberNotary takes more than just knowing the technology that is available, it takes self-respect, character, training, and ownership of the role of a Notary Public.

When a Notary Public respects him or herself, he or she will most likely respect others. Usually, Notary Public deals with people of different backgrounds, styles, culture, etc. More so now that our communities are becoming more diverse. Remember, a Notary Public's job is not to judge but to make sure that the signer is who the signer says he or she is.

Self-respect enhances the Notary's character. Seasoned Notaries have shared with me that many people, for unknown reasons, have tried to trick the Notary Public by presenting false documentation, by pretending that the spouse or relative wants to sign willingly when in reality the spouse or relative has been under coercion, or by rushing the signing process. A Notary's character must be willing to politely refuse to perform a notarial act when the Notary Public notices "red flags" in the process. Although many commissioned Notaries Public make their public office the profession that brings in their main source of income, they are trusted by their Secretary of State to perform the notarial job with integrity and responsibly. A Notary Public have to develop the ability to keep the ball in the Notary's court. The moment the Notary Public allows the signer to rush the process or to prevent the Notary Public from following all the steps a trained Notary Public takes during each and every notarial act performed, the Notary Public puts him or herself at risk of being involved in a fraudulent act or could miss an important required-by-law step in the process.

Self-respect and character will definitely impact the Notary's training process. Sometimes, it takes training to develop character and

16

self-respect. In the field of a Notary Public, training comes embedded with vision, character, and self-respect. Most notaries I know, including myself, have the vision to see the communities safe and prospering with opportunities for families to succeed. If paperwork is not done right, it ripples to the signer having to spend more money, invest more time in redoing the paperwork, delaying the process at another office, and causing a series of inconveniences to the signer and to everyone involved or who will be involved. Sometimes, the notarial act might take a little longer than expected, but it is worth taking the time to make sure the signers are who they say they are, and paperwork is done right.

Self-respect, character, and training, will definitely impact how the Notary Public owns his or her role as commissioned Public Officer. Once the Notary Public owns his or her role during notarial acts, while networking, during a friendly conversation, at home, at work, at an event, etc, the Notary Public will not only earn more credibility but also make a positive impact. It is all connected. Many may not be aware of, but a Notary's role is important. Maybe this is why history books reveals Notaries Public from the past belonged to an elite circle. Anytime I meet a new commissioned Notary, I see hope shining in our society.

Becoming a Remote/WebCam or, how I call it, CyberNotary, begins in a person's heart. J.C. Maxwell wrote in his book *21 Irrefutable Laws of Leadership:* "Commitment starts in the heart. Commitment is tested by action. Commitment opens the doors to possibilities." It is not different for a Notary Public. A Notary must be committed to do it right every time. Once committed, then, apply and follow through the application process.

What is an Electronic Notary Commission? It is the granted Commission that enables a commissioned Notary Public to conduct notarial acts electronically. It is important that a Notary Public does not confuse Electronic notarization with Remote/WebCam notarization. More about the difference between the two ahead.

How to become an Electronic Notary Public? Please, note that I am commissioned as an Electronic Notary Public in the Commonwealth of Virginia. In my case, I had to be commissioned as a Traditional Notary Public first. Even after becoming a traditional Notary Public, I had to take steps prior to applying for an Electronic Notary Public Commission. I had to obtain a Digital Certificate[3] and a Digital Seal[4] that had my name as it appears on my Commission as Traditional Notary Public, traditional registration number, and expiration date of my commission as Traditional Public Notary. The Commision of an Electronic Notary Public is more like an added bonus to the Traditional Notary Public Commission. They both expire at the same time.

In regards to the Digital Certificate. It is important that the Notary Public aspiring to become a Commissioned Electronic Notary research companies before selecting one. It is very important that the company that distributes Digital Certificates is trusted and verifiable by the office of the Secretary of State. I recommend *IdenTrust*.

What is a Digital Certificate? Is an encrypted digital tool that contains personal information tied to a specific Public Key Infrastructure (PKI) embedded with algorithm that, after it is created, it could be seen as a digital fingerprint. Visually, it does not look like a thumb fingerprint. It is more like a rectangular box with a bunch of codes. This type of certificate is issued by a Certifying Authority (CA) like *IdenTrust*. A Digital Certificate provides information about the identity of a person.

Why the need for a Digital Certificate? due to the openness of cyberspace, more rigorous measurements have to be taken when conducting legal transactions over the internet. At least Electronic Notaries Public aspirants in the Commonwealth of Virginia have to get a Digital Certificate and learn how to use it in order to complete the application process before the application reaches the office of the Secretary of the Commonwealth for approval.

It is important to notice that a Digital Certificate may expire earlier than the Notary Public Commission. For example, my Digital Certificate is valid for two years. My commission as Notary Public is valid for four years, and so is my electronic Notary Public commission. So, most likely, I will have to get a new Digital Certificate before my Commission as Public Notary expires.

---

[3] Digital Certificate: encrypted and verifiable identity.
[4] Digital Seal: Digital version of the Notary's wet-ink Seal.

Now, what is a Digital Seal and why use it? Just like a traditional notary public would stamp a document with a wet-ink seal, and Electronic Notary Public needs a Digital Seal to stamp the electronic document. Once again, at least it is this way in the Commonwealth of Virginia.

My Digital Seal has my name as it is registered in my Traditional Notary Public Commission, my traditional registration number, and the expiration date of my Traditional Notary Public Commision. My Digital Seal will be valid for four years expiring the same day my traditional Notary Public commision does.

Now you know that the Digital Certificate may expire in two years while the Digital Seal will remain valid for the time of your current Notary Public commision.

ALWAYS CHECK YOUR STATE OR COMMONWEALTH LAWS RELATED TO NOTARIAL ACTS and ELECTRONIC NOTARIAL ACTS.

Digital Certificate obtained and Digital Seal obtained. Now what? In the Commonwealth of Virginia, aspirants go to the website of the Secretary of the Commonwealth, open an application online, fill it out, sign it utilizing the Digital Certificate and the Digital Seal, and pay the required application fee. After that, it is just waiting for the final decision which is usually sent to the Commissioned Notary Public's e-mail on file. The wait for the answer could give the Electronic Notary Public aspirant enough time to put in practice traditional notarial acts, take courses, and get familiarized with relevant terms commonly used by electronic notaries public in the cyber-environment.

My Electronic Public Notary Commission was approved. Now what? Am I considered a Remote or WebCam Notary instantly? The answer depends on the Commissioned Notary Public. Being approved as an electronic Notary Public means that the commissioned Notary Public is now allowed to perform electronic notarial acts utilizing an electronic device such a computer in order to digitally sign documents. There is a very important difference when it comes to Electronic Notarization and Remote/WebCam Notarization. An Electronic Notarization does not necessarily need a built-in camera or external video camera to perform the notarization, while the Remote/WebCam Notarization does. This also means that for the signing of the documents during an electronic notarization that is local, the signer must be physically present, while in a remote/WebCam Notarization, which also implements electronic means, the signer must be present virtually in Real Time[5]. A pre-recorded version of the signer is not acceptable. It must be a live or Real Time encounter.

The note above about real time reminds me of my first Remote Notarization where I was the client. I was getting ready to move to Virginia from Oklahoma and I needed a PO BOX where all my mail could be forwarded to. I found a Virtual PO BOX service in Virginia which required a notarized document. When I contacted the company with the virtual service, the company referred me to a Remote Notary Public based in Virginia. I made an appointment with the Remote Notary. The day and time of the appointment arrived. I signed-on with the information provided by the Remote Notary Public, had my computer ready, web camera on, audio on, built-in mic on, and printer/scanner plugged-in to the computer. It was my first real time experience with a Remote Notary Public. It was what inspired me to become a Remote/Webcam Notary, or how I call it: a CyberNotary.

---

[5] Real Time: live presence, at the same time. Not pre-recorded.

Chapter 1: Review

-Notary Public dates back to 2750 BC.

-At least in the Commonwealth of Virginia, anyone aspiring to be commissioned as Electronic Notary Public must apply and be commissioned as a Traditional Notary Public first.

-Becoming a CyberNotary takes more than just knowing the technology that is available, it takes self-respect, character, training, and ownership of the role of a Notary Public.

-What a Notary Public does or omits on a document today is as good today as it will be in the future.

-A main Notary Public's job is not to judge but to make sure the signers are who they say they are.

-A Notary must be willing to politely refuse to perform a notarial act when the Notary Public notices "red flags" in the process.

-In the field of a Notary Public, training comes embedded with vision, character, and self-respect.

-Most likely, a person interested in becoming a Remote/WebCam Notary will have to apply for an Electronic Notary Commision.

-Most likely, before a person can apply for an Electronic Notary Public Commission, the person has to be commissioned as Traditional Notary Public first. (At least, in the Commonwealth of Virginia it is that way).

-A Digital Certificate is an encrypted digital tool that contains personal information tied to a specific Public Key Infrastructure (PKI) embedded with algorithms.

-A Digital Seal is a version of the Traditional Seal that contains the Notary's registered name, registration number, expiration date, and the State or Commonwealth where the Notary Public is Commissioned at.

-In a local electronic notarization the signer must be physically present.

-In a Remote/WebCam notarization, the signer must be virtually present in real time.

-The recommended minimum hardware for both the Remote Notary and the Remote Signer are: well maintained computer with access to the internet (high speed preferably), functional speakers, functional microphone, functional webcam, functional printer and scanner plugged in to the computer, printing paper.

Chapter 2: Digital Certificate & Digital Seal

Digital Certificate: in the case of utilizing a Digital Certificate to sign a document, the type of Digital Certificate used is not a certificate similar to a paper certificate in which a person is recognized for an accomplishment. It is a Digital Certificate that has digital encryption embedded with algorithms that verify the notary's identity and, in this context, allows the Notary Public to exchange information over the internet using a Public Key Infrastructure (PKI). This Digital Certificate is generated and provided by a Certifying Authority (CA) such as *IdenTrust*.

For example, if the Remote or WebCam notary decides to use Adobe products when retrieving and signing documents, at the moment of signing, the notary will sign with the Digital Certificate instead of signing with a preformatted signature or a signature created by the notary. The notary will retrieve the Digital Certificate which should be stored either in a ThumbDrive provided by the Certifying Authority or another form of storage authentication also provided by a Certifying Authority.

The Digital Certificate pretty much replaces notary's wet signature or Notary's self-created signature providing a more secured transaction in a cyber-environment.
A Digital Certificate is not free and it is not cheap either. However, when reflecting on the security it provides, the amount is well worth investing in.

Digital Seal: after a document has been signed with a Digital Certificate, most likely the Notary Public will need to stamp the document with the Notarial Seal that contains the Notary's name as registered in the commision, the valid registration number, expiration date, and State or Commonwealth where the notary public is commissioned at.
At least in the Commonwealth of Virginia, in order to comply with the law, a Digital Seal must be used even if the digital document has already been signed with a Digital Certificate.

An electronic notary can order a Digital Seal at:
https://www.acornsales.com/Notary-Eseal-p/3008-n.htm?gclid=CjwKCAj w7cDaBRBtEiwAsxprXQtNDXbfs8Q3BIzCIUruMGt1h83iCpGVuMgwP BamtTgkbZXoazktNxoCA5MQAvD_BwE&gdffi=ed868725a66948178b 98906202f43708&gdfms=61C1643F6BC3413EA417BAF18FE728B8

Digital Seals are also known as eSeals. The notary must take into consideration the photographically reproduction of the Seal to comply with the law in places such as the Commonwealth of Virginia. As an experienced in digital photography, I recommend that the minimum of your eSeal is designed with a 300 dots per inch (dpi) printable capacity. This way, if the document has to be printed, the eSeal will print clearly, not blurry or of low identifiable quality.
Today, dpi is usually confused with ppi (pixel per inch). In the Notary Public world, you want your seals to be photographically reproduced or clear when printed; therefore, the notary wants to refer to the photographically reproducible eSeal in dots per inch (dpi).

Most likely, the company who generates the Notary's eSeal will e-mail the completed eSeals in more than one format: jpg and TIFF.

JPG and JPEG are used interchangeably.
It stands for *Joint Photographic Experts Group*.
TIFF and TIF are also used interchangeably in digital
environments. It stands for *Tag Image File Format*.

As previously mentioned, the eSeal, most likely will
be e-mailed to the Notary when it is completed. A way
to safeguard the eSeal is by storing it in a password-
protected folder that only the Notary Public has access to.

Visual Sample of a verifiable Digital Certificate and eSeal:

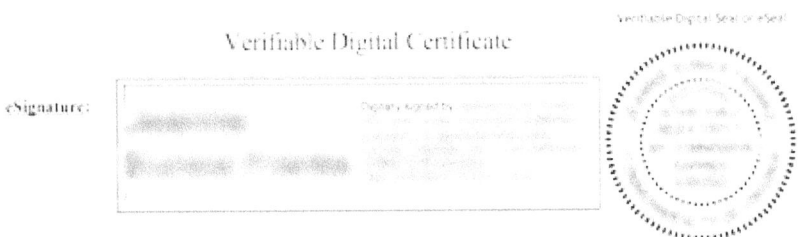

Chapter 2: Review

- A Digital Certificate is a verifiable certificate generated and provided by a Certifying Authority (CA). It has digital encryption embedded with algorithms that verifies the notary's identity, and thanks to a Public Key Infrastructure (PKI), the Notary Public is able to make secure transactions over the internet.

- A Digital Certificate may be stored in a ThumbDrive provided by the Certifying Authority.

- The Digital Certificate replaces the notary's wet signature or Notary's self-created signature providing a more secured transaction in the cyber-environment.

- A Notarial Seal contains the Notary's name as registered in the commision, the valid registration number, expiration date, and the State or Commonwealth where the notary public is commissioned at.

- A Digital Certificate may expire in two years while the Digital Seal expires at the same time the Traditional Notary Public commission expires.

- The Remote Notary Public must verify the laws of his/her State or Commonwealth to see of a Digital is necessary to comply with the laws of that State or Commonwealth.

- The Digital Seal is the same as the Traditional Notary Public Seal but digital and provided by companies such as acornsales.com.

- Digital Seals are also known as eSeals.

- It is recommended that the minimum of the eSeal has a 300 dots per inch (dpi) printable capacity.

- Eseals may be e-mailed to the Notary in, at least, two formats: JPEG also known as JPG, or TIFF also known as TIF.

- Since the eSeal is e-mailed and downloadable, the Notary Public wants to save it in a password-protected file and environment.

Chapter 3: Proper Remote/WebCam Notarization

I believe that in order for a Remote/WebCam Notarization to be proper, the first thing a Notary Public must take care of is safety in a holistic way; from the safety of the Notary to the security of the transactions that will take place.

If the Notary is conducting business remotely from home, the safety of the Notary shall not be of concern. However, if the remote notarization will be conducted from a place away from home, then, the Notary must take certain precautions:

-If remote notarization will take place away from home, make sure transportation is taken care of. Do not wait until the last minute to fill up the gas tank, change the oil, or replace a tire. If given a ride, make sure the driver will not be at risk of getting a DUI.[6]

-Make sure the place where the remote notarization will be conducted at is safe; with minimal unexpected situations that could put the mobile remote eNotary in danger.

-If away from home while performing remote/WebCam notarizations, have basic essentials at hand such as a bottle of water, protein bar or fruits, etc; anything that will serve as sustenance. A Remote notarization should not take too long, but one never knows. An eNotary wants to always have a clear mind and be aware of surroundings. An eNotary must always do the best to be safe.

Another important point is to be ontime. A Remote/WebCam notary wants to always increase reliability and credibility. Being late to an online appointment with a client could make a negative impact; the client might not want to proceed with the transaction or the Remote/WebCam Notary might not be requested again by that client.

---

[6] DUI: Driving under the influence.

At home or away from home, a Remote/WebCam Notary wants to have access to all the required notarial tools. Functional Computer, Digital Certificate, Digital Seal, access to an Electronic Journal if logging electronic notarial acts is required by law in the state or Commonwealth the Notary is commissioned at, passwords for the account that will be used to process the digital signing, a functional web camera, printer/scanner in case there is a need for it, knowledge of how to proceed, notes and phone numbers of trusted people such as someone from a Notary Association that could mentor the Notary in case of doubt, the Notary Handbook of the State or Commonwealth where the Notary is commissioned at, cable chargers for computer, cellphone, and other devices the Remote Notary makes use of during Remote/WebCam notarial acts, if the computer does not have a built-in microphone, then a microphone compatible with the computer, any peripheral that the Remote/WebCam notary utilizes during remote notarizations. Some notaries use external hard-drives to secure information. Even if the notary is the only one touching the equipment, having hands sanitized everytime the notary utilizes the computer, mouse, etc is a good habit to preserve. Include a hand sanitizer.

Remote/WebCam/Online notaries must follow the steps required by the platform they are using, and implement traditional notary public guidelines as well. This is why it is very important that the web cameras the Notary and the client are using have good visual resolution. Just like a signing in person where the Notary Public takes a real good look at the client who is physically present, a Remote Notary wants to be able to do the same virtually. The client must be virtually present in real time and have access to a web camera that reads pixels clearly.

Remote Notaries are privileged right now because the demand and supply for audiovisual equipment has increased. Price of audiovisual equipment with good digital resolution compatible with most computers available in the general market has decreased.

Notaries who have Mac[7] computers, have an advantage and a disadvantage. Most Mac equipment tends to be more expensive than most of the other kind. However, a Notary who have a MacBook Pro, for example, knows that the computer comes with a very good built-in camera. So, when making the appointment with the client, let the client know that he or she needs access to a computer with a good Web-Camera built-in or plugged-in to it. Notaries want to be able to compare the Identification provided by the client with the client who must be present in real time. It is recommended to provide specific instructions to the client prior to the appointment time.

---

[7] Mac from Apple Inc.

Chapter 3: Review

- The first thing a Notary Public must take care of is safety in a holistic way.

- Safety of the Notary shall not be of concern when conducting Remote notarizations from home.

- The Notary Public must take precautions when conducting notarial business away from home. Certain aspects must be previously taken care of such as transportation, pre-screening of the location where the remote notarial act will take place. If riding as passenger, the Notary wants to make sure the driver has not consumed illegal substances or too much alcohol. The Notary wants to have some kind of sustenance in case the remote notarial act takes longer than expected.

- A mobile eNotary wants to always have a clear mind and awareness of the surroundings where the remote notarial act takes place.

- A mobile eNotary must always do the best to be safe.

- Remote/WebCam Notary Public wants to be ontime to online appointments.

- A Remote/WebCam Notary wants to have access and control over all his/hers required notarial tools and make sure all the tools are functional prior to performing notarial acts.

-     Traditional Notary Public training is the foundation of every notarial act including Remote/WebCam notarizations. It is recommended that the Notary and the client have access to web cameras that record and broadcast clear images.

- The WebCam Notary wants to make sure the client appears online in real time in order to compare the valid identification provided by the client.

- Notaries want to take time identifying the signer as if it was a traditional notarization.

Jeannie Eunice Franks

Chapter 4: Safeguarding Digital Notarial Tools

Once the Notary becomes an electronic Notary with the capacity to provide Remote/WebCam/Online notarizations, the notary gains a new level of responsibility in cyberspace; the notary becomes a digital counter-entity of fraudulent intentions with the ability to politely refuse to provide notarial acts when "red flags[8]" have been detected by the Remote/WebCam Notary.

What are Digital Notarial Tools? The resources with digital access needed to complete Remote/WebCam notarizations; for example, the computer being one of the main resources. A Notary wants to safeguard the electronic equipment he or she uses during remote notarial acts. If and when possible, the notary should be the only one with "Administrator permission[9]" to the computer he or she uses during remote notarial acts. I am not much of approval of notaries who utilize electronic equipment owned by other people or electronic equipment stationed at public places. At all times, Notaries must be able to have control over the equipment they use during electronic notarial acts.

Safeguarding digital notarial tools also means maintaining the hardware and software. The notary wants to keep the computer and its peripherals clean, away from dust or weather that could damage the equipment. The Notary wants to keep the interior environment of the computer defragmented, organized, updated with the latest version of antivirus, firewalls turned-on, and free from unnecessary programs occupying digital space and memory.

---

[8] Red Flags: a sign of something suspicious or wrong.
[9] The user with permission to access all files and make changes in the computer.

The notary wants to secure the hardware where the Digital Certificate has been stored not only to prevent unauthorized use of it but also to prevent the loss of it prompting the notary to have to report it to the Secretary of State and having to invest more money in another Digital Certificate.

A Remote/WebCam/Online Notary Public, in no way, is less than a Traditional Notary Public. On the contrary, it is the same but with enhanced possibilities and responsibilities.

The Notary wants to keep notarial tools away from the reach of children, other adults, and pets. It is the responsibility of the Notary to keep control over all the notarial-related equipment, logbooks, and dedicated space whether at home or away from home.

Chapter 4: Review

- What are Digital Notarial Tools? The resources with digital access needed to complete Remote/WebCam notarizations.

- If and when possible, the notary should be the only one with "administrator permission[10]" to the computer/laptop he or she uses during remote/notarial acts.

- Notaries must be able to have control over the equipment they use during electronic notarial acts.

- Safeguarding digital notarial tools also means maintaining the hardware and software.

- The Notary wants to keep the computer and its peripherals clean, away from dust or weather that could damage the equipment.

- The Notary wants to keep the interior environment of the computer defragmented, organized, updated with the latest version of antivirus, firewalls turned-on, and free from unnecessary programs occupying digital space and computer memory.

- The Notary wants to secure the hardware where the Digital Certificate has been stored.

- The Notary wants to keep notarial tools away from the reach of children, other adults, and pets.

---

[10] The user with permission to access all files and make changes in the computer.

Jeannie Eunice Franks

Chapter 5: Why Joining a Notary Public Association?

In my experience, joining a Notary Public Association has been one of the most helpful action I have taken as a commissioned Notary Public. As a member, I have not only enjoyed discounts on must-have notarial tools, but also has given me access to a network of resources from the seasoned and freshman in the field of notarial acts.

It is also known that laws might change or be amended every year. The Association keeps me up-to-date with changes or variations in the law that affect notarial acts.

Being connected to a resourceful network brings a great advantage to the Notary Public who joins the Association. Thanks to advances in technology, now notary networks are able to interact almost in real time no matter where a Notary may be at as long as internet, phone, and satellite signal are available.

A Notary Public does not have to be alone out there performing notarial duties without back-ups or mentorship. Being part of an Association brings all kinds of benefits to its members. Do not hesitate to join a Notary Association once your Commission as Notary Public has been approved. The field of notary public services continues to transcend to new platforms that all notaries should be aware of, specially the notaries who are willing to become electronic/Remote/WebCam/Online notaries.

Here are a few of the most known and respected Notary Associations known today in the United States of America:

National Notary Association (NNA)
https://www.nationalnotary.org/

American Association of Notaries
https://secure.usnotaries.net/members/Default.asp

American Society of Notaries
https://www.asnnotary.org/

American Notary USA
https://americannotaryusa.com/

Chapter 5: Review

-A Notary Public does not have to be alone out there performing notarial duties without back-ups or mentorship.

-Thanks to advances in technology, now notary networks are able to interact almost in real time no matter where a Notary may be at as long as internet, phone, and satellite signals are available.

-Four known and respected Notary Associations:

National Notary Association (NNA)
American Association of Notaries
American Society of Notaries
American Notary USA

Chapter 6: Why Continue Notary Public Education?

Recently, I took a class designed to enhance basic Notary Public knowledge. Although I was familiar with its content, it served as an excellent refresher. Little details are big details when they are taken into consideration in a court case. If you are new in the business, take a course. If you are a seasoned notary, take a refresher course. It is normal to get comfortable. Sometimes, within the comfort zone, little details are forgotten or overlooked. Attention to detail is one of the founding principles of performing a notarial act right every time. Refresher courses serve much in a Notary's journey.

It seems that due to current transitions happening in the notarial field, more courses are available online and more venues seem to be available for in-classroom education. Just recently, I found out that bill 1343 passed in the Commonwealth of Virginia. This Bill has to do with employers, fees, and the employee who happens to be a Notary Public as well. The post can be found at https://www.virginianotary.club/blog/bill1343.

In my experience, one never stops learning. Even the least curious grasps something in the way. The field that wraps a Notary Public is open to grasping not only from new technologies, amended laws, new laws, changes in the notarial law, but also from the diverse community that a Notary Public has the opportunity to provide notarial services to. A Notary Public education never ceases to ask for more or to ask for a refresher. Each layer of education navigated by a Notary Public requires reviews as often as possible. Many may not understand it this way because, to some, a Notary Public service is not as lucrative. Remember, a Notary Public is also a Public Officer abiding by the State or Commonwealth laws where his or her commission has been granted. As Notary Public, there is more than charging a fee for a notarial act; as such, a Notary Public serves an entire State or Commonwealth where demographics may vary along with cultural values. A Notary Public has the opportunity to become an expert at reading people from all backgrounds. This is a must in order to detect fraud or coercion beyond the face printed clearly on a valid identification.

LAYERS OF EDUCATION IN A NOTARY'S JOURNEY

How to become a Notary Public?

What is a Seal?

What is an embosser?

How a document is stamped?

How to maintain the Notary tools?

How much money is it required to invest in order to have access to all the required notarial tools?

What are the Notary Laws in the State or Commonwealth where the commission was approved?

How to keep a Notary LogBook (also known as Notary Journal)?

How many types of Notary Public exist?

What is the legal language of Notarial acts?

What vocabulary is required to absorb as a Notary Public?

Why is the job of a Notary Public important?

What is E & O insurance?

What is a bond?

What is the difference between Windows PC and a MAC?

What internet speed is necessary for a clear online notarization?

What Web Camera is best for Remote notarial acts?

What other devices are recommended for electronic notarizations?

What are Acrobat Products?

What are the recommended steps to follow during notarial acts?

What is a Digital Certificate?

What is an Electronic Seal?

How much does it cost to be an electronic Notary Public?

Here are quick answers to the previous questions:

How to become a Notary Public?
Visit your Secretary of State online page. The Commonwealth of Virginia Secretary of State for Notary Applications is:
https://www.commonwealth.virginia.gov/official-documents/notary-commissions/

What is a Seal?
It is the inked impression stamped that authenticate the Notary's signature during a notarial act.

What is an embosser?
It is an elevated impression of the Seal on a Document. Usually, it does not have any color, and many Notaries use Gold Stickers to stamp with an embosser as a final touch after stamping with the photographically reproductive Seal.

How is a document stamped?
Generally, the seal is placed next to the Notary's signature without obstructing any other wording in the document.

How to maintain the Notary tools?
Keep them clean, free of dust, secured, out of the reach of children, other adults, and pets.

How much money is it required to invest in order to have access to all the required notarial tools?
When a Notary joins a Notary Association, savings may occur. Have in mind that a Traditional Notary needs, at least, to pay for the Notary application fee which may vary in each State, stamps, Notary LogBook, pens, etc. If the Notary becomes mobile and electronic, a dual trace laser printer might be needed, a laptop, access to the internet, a smart phone, webcam, etc.

If the notary already have access to the electronic equipment. Then, the Notary might need an investment budget of $400, at least in the year 2018.

What are the Notary Laws in the State or Commonwealth where the commission was approved?
It may vary by State or Commonwealth. Check the Secretary of State's website and look for the current Notary Handbook.

How to keep a Notary LogBook (also known as Notary Journal)?
Keep it clean and secured. Also, document as much information as possible in the LogBook. If a court case requires information from the Notary, the LogBook is the best place the Notary will be able to find it.

How many types of Notary Public exist?
Traditional, Mobile, Electronic, Remote (also known as WebCam and Online Notaries).

What is the legal language of Notarial acts?
In United States of America, it is English. The Notary wording in a document must always be written or stamped in the English language.

What vocabulary is required in the Notary Public field?
There are many words that are not used in the everyday life such as Jurat.

Why is the job of a Notary Public important?
Notaries has been part of society for centuries and their job helps society move forward while, at the same time, notaries have a big role in deterring fraudulent intentions.

What is E & O insurance?
Is a type of insurance that protects the Notary.

What is a bond?
Is a type of insurance that protects clients against the negligence of notaries.

What is the difference between Windows PC and a MAC?
They use different operating Systems.

What internet speed is necessary for a clear online notarization?
high speed internet connection (T1 or DSL) and have at least 1.6 GHz of processing speed with 512 MB RAM. It is not only the internet speed but also the computer processing speed and memory.

What Web Camera is best for Remote notarial acts?
Some laptops already come with a reasonable built-in web-camera. However, if the notary is buying an external camera, a recommended one would be a camera with a least 720p.
1080p is best.

What other devices are recommended for electronic notarizations?
I recommend having Adobe Acrobat installed. Adobe Pro DC is my favorite. Also, more electronic notaries are entering the field of Title closing and mortgages. Having a Dual tray laser printer and a multi-document scanner would be helpful. Cover the basic first; Digital Certificate, Digital Seal, laptop or desktop, Adobe Acrobat, smart phone, E & O insurance, if the State or Commonwealth requires a Bond, then, a Bond, and the basic marketing materials.

What are Acrobat Products?
They are applications that let users read, fill-out, sign, and manage portable documents formats (PDF). My Favorite is Adobe Pro DC.

What are the recommended steps to follow during notarial acts?
Traditionally, it is recommended that the Notary identify the
signer first, then, look at the document to be notarized. Before
performing the notarial act, the notary fills out the notary's LogBook
or journal allowing opportunity to compare signatures since the signer
also has to sign the LogBook. After that, proceed with the
notarization. The idea is to provide enough space in time to make
sure the signer is who he or she says he or she is. Now, when it comes
to Remote notarizations, it is important to be ontime to the online
appointment and have all the equipment and documents ready. Before
notarizing electronically, it is necessary that the notary takes a good
look at the person behind the camera and make sure the person is
present in real time. Have the remote client show the identification
again live on camera, etc.

What is a Digital Certificate?
It is a verifiable certificate generated and provided by a Certifying
Authority (CA). It has digital encryption embedded with algorithms
that verifies the notary's identity, and thanks to a Public Key
Infrastructure (PKI), the Notary Public is able to make secure
transactions over the internet.

What is an Electronic Seal?
Interestingly, sometimes the electronic seal is confused with an
electronic signature. It is not the same. An electronic signature could
be the name of a person written digitally, like a signature on a pad
at a grocery store. An Electronic Seal or Digital Seal is the digital
version of the Notary's stamp that contains the Notary's name as
it appears in the commision, registration number, expiration date,
and State or Commonwealth replacing the wet ink stamp for the
digital one.

What is a Digital Signature?

In the digital environment, it is known that a Digital Signature could be considered the Digital Certificate of the notary. When the word "Digital is involved", there is more security involved when compared to the word "electronic." A Notary wants to have a Digital Certificate or Digital Seal or Digital Signature. It is always recommended to check the laws of the State or Commonwealth to make sure what it is required.

There is always something to learn or something to review in order to refresh the memory and continue to polish the work that it is done as Notary Public. Digitally or electronically, knowledge, care, attention to detail are embedded together. Notary Education is constantly adding ways to bring in tools that will help notaries polish their notarial acts. Anytime notaries can, notaries should take a course, a refresher one, or a course that will sharpen and expand notarial boundaries.

Here are a few known and well respected Organizations that offer online and in-classroom education for notaries:

https://www.nationalnotary.org
http://www.vanotaryedu.com
https://atgschools.com/notary
https://www.notarylearningcenter.com
http://www.thenotarybusinessschool.com
https://www.waketech.edu
https://www.pgcc.edu/Programs_and_Courses/Noncredit/Continuing_Education_Program_Detail.aspx?id=6442462736

Chapter 6: Review

-Little details are big details when they are taken into consideration in a court case.

-If you are new in the notary business, take a course. If you are a seasoned notary, take a refresher course.

-Each layer of education navigated by a Notary Public requires reviews as often as possible.

-A Notary Public is also a Public Officer abiding by the State or Commonwealth laws where his or her commission has been granted.

-The first step to become a Notary Public is to be motivated and visit your Secretary of State online page. The Commonwealth of Virginia Secretary of State for Notary Applications is:
https://www.commonwealth.virginia.gov/official-documents/notary-commissions/

-A seal is the inked impression stamped that authenticate the Notary's signature during a notarial act.

-Embosser is an elevated impression of the Seal on a Document.

-Generally, a document is stamped by placing the seal next to the Notary's signature without obstructing any other wording in the document.

-There is an investment to be made when becoming a commissioned Notary Public. It is of good practice to join a Notary Association not only for savings but also for educational purposes, support, and other benefits.

-The laws may vary by State or Commonwealth. Check the Secretary of State's website and look for the current Notary Handbook. Also check with the Notary Association.

-It is also of good practice to keep the Notary LogBook clean and secured. Also, document as much information as possible in the LogBook. If a court case requires information from the Notary, the LogBook is the best place the Notary will be able to find it.

-There are a variety of Notaries Public: Traditional, Mobile, Electronic, Remote (also known as WebCam and Online notaries).

-According to the Virginia Notary Handbook, the legal language of notary wording in The United States of America is English. The Notary wording in a document must always be written or stamped in the English language.

-The job of a Notary Public is important because it helps society move forward while, at the same time, notaries have a big role in deterring fraudulent intentions.

-The Errors & Omission insurance (E&O insurance) is a type of insurance that protects the Notary.

-A bond is a type of insurance that protects clients against the negligence of notaries.

-High speed internet is recommended during online notarizations.

-A recommended web-camera would be a camera with a least 720p or 1080p which is best.

-Adobe products are applications that let users read, fill-out, sign, and manage portable documents formats (PDF).

-The recommended steps to follow during notarial acts are:
greet and identify the signer, eye-scan the document to be notarized,
open and fill out the notary logbook or journal, ask the signer to sign
the logbook, proceed with notarizing the document, stay alert for
signs of coercion or fraudulent intentions. When notarizing online,
make sure the signer is present in real time, the video is clear, and
audio free of unwanted noise.

-A Digital Certificate is a verifiable certificate generated and provided
by a Certifying Authority (CA). It has digital encryption embedded
with algorithms that verifies the notary's identity, and thanks to a
Public Key Infrastructure (PKI), the Notary Public is able to make
secured transactions over the internet.

-An Electronic Seal or Digital Seal is the digital version of the
Notary's official stamp.

-Anytime notaries can, notaries should take a course, a refresher one,
or a course that will sharpen and expand notarial boundaries.

Chapter 7: Digital Platforms for Notaries

With new digital platforms available for notarial acts, it is highly recommended that notaries begin to familiarize with those platforms in order to decide which one will suit better the service and ability to handle online notarizations. Like most of other disciplines, it is a matter of practice. Once the Notary finds a digital platform that suits him or her well, then practice, practice, practice and familiarize with the vocabulary implemented in that particular platform. Moreover, some companies have their own platform.

Here are a few platforms that are already known by most eNotaries:

Safedocs
Snapdocs
DocVerify
DocuSign
Notarize
NotaryCam
SIGNiX
DocMagic
NotarySoftware

Here are a few companies that have the capability to add Notaries to their Network and that provide their own selected digital platforms:

http://www.pavaso.com
https://notary.solidifi.com
https://app.notarize.com/login
https://www.notarysoftware.com
https://www.docmagic.com
https://www.theclosingexchange.com

What is a Digital Platform? Is is the software or designed digital environment where users interact digitally. For example, Facebook is a digital Platform. Programs such as *Notarize, PAVASO, Snapdocs, Quora, Google, Instagram, LinkedIn, Twitter, Instagram, YouTube, Amazon, Ebay, Snapchat* are also considered digital platforms.

There are different types of Digital Platforms: Social, Knowledge, Media, Repository, Infrastructure, Classifieds, Application Stores, Market Places, Crowd-Sourcing, and others designed with a functional purpose online. A lot of Digital Platforms are advertising driven.

In my experience, the digital platforms I have used to conduct notarial acts online have been straight to the point without distracting pop-ups or links directing me to an ad. From my perspective, online signings seem more secure that way; no ads, no third parties self-inviting themselves to private online transactions.

As a Remote/WebCam/Online Notary, the notary wants to keep the work to the point; filling out what is necessary, identifying signers, digitally stamping, etc. Although Customer Service is important to build rapport and to win trust from clients, the Remote notary wants to be time-efficient. The role of a Remote Notary completing an order through a Digital Platform designed to facilitate online notary services is that of a Notary not of a Facebook friend nor of a marketer at a public chat room.

Once the Notary becomes a Commissioned Electronic Notary Public, he or she is able to provide Remote/WebCam notarizations if allowed in the State or Commonwealth where the commission was granted.

Even in the online environment, a Notary Public must be respectful, time-efficient, computer savvy, keep a professional attitude and image when interacting with clients and the companies the Notary is doing the online notarizations for. Remember, the Notary is not only representing himself or herself, it is representing a system, and a State or Commonwealth of the United States of America.

Chapter 7: Review

-Digital Platforms are software or designed digital environments where users interact digitally most likely in cyberspace.

-There are different types of Digital Platforms: Social, Knowledge, Media, Repository, Infrastructure, Classifieds, Application Stores, Market Places, Crowd-Sourcing, and others designed with a functional purpose online.

-The Remote notary wants to be time-efficient.

-Even in the online environment, a Notary Public must be respectful, time-efficient, computer savvy, keep a professional attitude and image when interacting with clients and the companies the Notary is doing the online notarizations for.

Jeannie Eunice Franks

Chapter 8: Basic Vocabulary for Remote/WebCam Notaries

Before entering in the digital environment, let remember some common types of Notarial Acts:

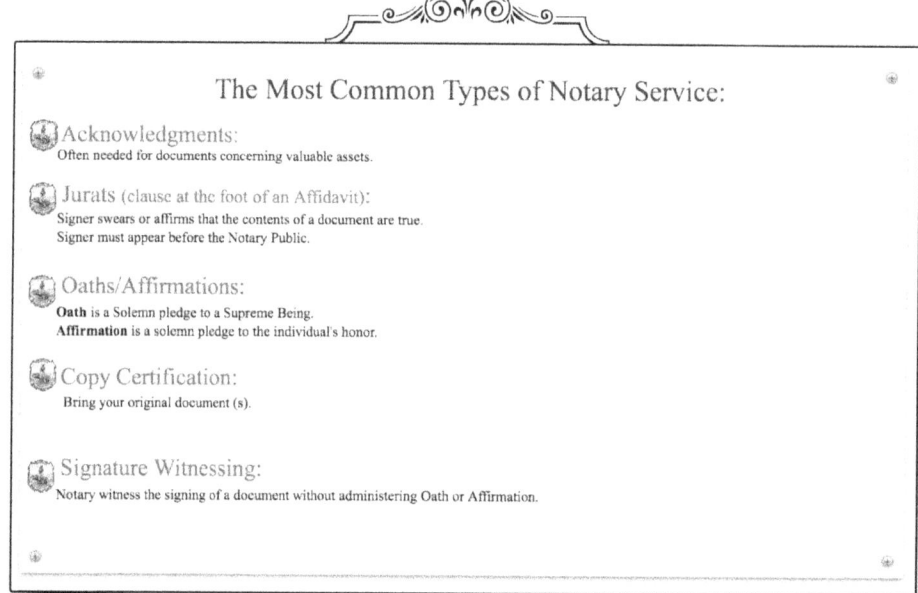

The Most Common Types of Notary Service:

Acknowledgments:
Often needed for documents concerning valuable assets.

Jurats (clause at the foot of an Affidavit):
Signer swears or affirms that the contents of a document are true.
Signer must appear before the Notary Public.

Oaths/Affirmations:
Oath is a Solemn pledge to a Supreme Being.
Affirmation is a solemn pledge to the individual's honor.

Copy Certification:
Bring your original document (s).

Signature Witnessing:
Notary witness the signing of a document without administering Oath or Affirmation.

7 items that must be taken care of during each

Notarial Act in the Commonwealth of Virginia

I am adding these items here because it might be useful to notaries in other states. However, always, always, always, check the laws of the State or Commonwealth where the notary's commission has been granted. According to the current Commonwealth of Virginia Notary Handbook, the 7 items that must be taken care of during each notarial act are:

1. Notarial statement
2. The date of the notarial act
3. The location of the notarial act in the city or county where notarization occurs
4. The expiration date of the notary's commission
5. Notary's signature
6. Notary's registration number
7. Photographically reproducible notary seal/stamp

As Remote/WebCam notaries commissioned in the Commonwealth of Virginia, item number 5 would be the Digital Certificate, and item number 7 would be the Digital Seal.

During a Remote notarial act, item number 3 is the location where the Remote/WebCam Notary is located at the time of notarization. For example, the Remote Notary is located in the city of Hampton,Virginia, and the client is located in Richmond, Virginia. The location that is recorded in both the document and the electronic journal is Hampton, VA.

Basic Vocabulary
for Remote/WebCam Notaries

Digital Certificate	A verifiable digital identity, portable via PKI, and provided by a Certifying Authority.
Digital Seal	The digital version of the wet Notary's Stamp.
Digital Platform	Digital interactive environment designed with a purpose to be deployable in cyberspace.
SmartPhone	A mobile phone with the capability to modify, create, receive, and send data over the internet wirelessly beside making phone calls.
Electronic Notary	Commissioned Notary allowed to sign documents electronically also known as eNotary.
Remote/WebCam Notary	Commissioned Notary able to conduct notarial acts virtually utilizing a Web-Camera and microphone.
Mobile eNotary	Notary Public available and willing to travel away from home or office in order to conduct notarial acts electronically.
Certifying Authority	The entity authorized to provide Digital Certificates.
Pixels	A very small area of light on a digital screen.
Dots Per Inch (dpi)	Printable measurement of an image; the output resolution of a printed image.
PDF	Portable Document Format widely used when sharing or sending documents online.
JPEG or JPG	Digital compressing format for images.
TIFF or TIF	Tag Image File Format usually used to store graphics.

Electronic Journal	Electronic version of the Notary's journal or LogBook.
Real Time	the "now" time or actual time when the notarization takes place.
Venue	In the case of Remote Notarization, it is the location where the Remote Notary is at when the notarization occurs.
Network	Connection. Interconnectedness of people, systems, or things.
Dual Tray Laser Printer	The recommended printer for eNotaries that are loan closers and provide services in the mortgage system.
URL	Stands for Uniform Resource Locator. It is the address in the world Wide Web.
Username	The word or name selected when signing-in. There are cases that the username is an entire e-mail.
Password	The private combination of letters, numbers, and or special characters that grants access to protected information or online membership.
Apps	Short for "Applications." In this case are considered downloadable software.
eClosing	The process is done electronically and documents remain in their electronic form.
Digital vs Electronic	Think of Digital Signature vs Electronic Signature. The first one uses PKI technology. The latter one does not.
PKI	Public Key Infrastructure that supports the distribution and identification of public encryption keys, enabling users and computers to both securely exchange data over networks such as the Internet and verify the identity of the other party. (Whatis.com)
Electronic Certificate	It is the area in the electronic document completed by the Notary Public that includes the notarial wording and the Notary's official digital seal.

Chapter 8: Review

-Common types of notarial acts: Acknowledgements, Jurats, Oath/Affirmation, Copy Certification, and Signature Witnessing.

-At least in the Commonwealth of Virginia, there are seven items that must always be taken care of during every notarial act: notarial statement, date of notarial act, venue or location where the notarial act took place, expiration date of the notary's commission, notary's signature, notary's registration number, and the stamping of a photographically reproducible seal.

-During a Remote notarial act, the location that is recorded in the document and Notary's logbook is the city or county where the Remote Notary is located at during the notarization.

-Words to remember: Digital Certificate Digital Seal, Digital Platform, SmartPhone, Electronic Notary, Remote/WebCam Notary, Mobile eNotary, Certifying Authority, Pixels, Dots per inches (dpi), PDF, JPEG, TIFF, Electronic Journal, Real Time, Venue, Network, Dual Tray Laser Printer, URL, Username, Password, Apps, eClosing, PKI, Electronic Certificate.

Jeannie Eunice Franks

Chapter 9: Basic Computer and SmartPhone Skills

Without basic computer skills, a Remote/WebCam Notary Public would have a hard time accomplishing tasks. Now-a-day, computers and smartphones function very similarly. Notaries on-the-go have to be connected and technologically adept or be able to adapt to the changes in technology that influence the way enabled notaries run their notary business. Moreover, conducting notarial acts from a laptop or desktop computer requires an added level of care traditional-only-notaries do not have to think about; an added level of security.

It is known that the internet is more than just a cloud, it is an open universe without real boundaries or jurisdictions. Every time a person turns on a computer or smartphone and connects the device to the internet, data has open doors to come in and out. Notaries Public have to implement extra security measurements in order to protect the data that they deal with when conducting notarial acts online. Also, due to the nature of the notary's role, a Remote/WebCam Notary, technically, becomes an online fraud-deterrent agent. It all starts by making sure that the equipment the online notary uses to conduct notarial acts is secured and well taken care of. Moreover, it helps when the online notary knows and understands how to utilize the hardware and the <u>required</u> already installed software.

What is hardware? It is the tangible parts of the computer and smartphone.

What is software? It is the intangible elements included in the computer package. For example, the operating system such as windows 10 is a software. The programs installed such as Adobe Acrobat, Microsoft Office, etc, are also considered software. In a smartphone, the software is recognized as the apps already installed or the downloaded ones by the mobile users. The signal is intangible but it is a signal not a software. Audio is intangible, but it is not a software, it is just audio.

Laptop or desktop, Android or iPhone, keeping updated the software installed in the hardware and protected with the latest compatible antivirus are only basic ways to enhance security during notarial acts conducted via the electronic devices mentioned above.

If the enabled electronic Notary Public knows that computer skills are not his or her best attribute, taking computer courses would be appropriate. Waiting to learn how to use a computer and efficiently handle a smartphone could impact the required layers of security needed during online notarial acts. It could also impact time-efficiency during online notarizations. I have known commissioned notaries that started their notarial journey late in life and were not computer savvy. They had to make a decision: provide traditional notarial services only or enhance their technical computer skills in order to enter cyberspace as online notaries.
It was really up to each Notary Public. Some took a course, others decided to provide paper and wet-ink notarial services only.

As basic understanding of handling electronic documents, Adobe Products are a great resource. I believe Adobe Products are the most popular when dealing with online documents. Adobe Products are compatible with Windows and Mac OS (OS is the acronym for Operating System). Getting the compatible version will help. There are free courses online that teaches how to use Adobe Products.

Most new computers and smartphones already are wi-fi and bluetooth compatible. Wi-fi receives the signal that allows the software installed in the computer or smartphone to connect to the internet while bluetooth, when turned-on, enables connectivity with other devices nearby. For example, many printers are now bluetooth ready, so instead of having it plugged-in to a computer, the printers, once configured, receive the signal or command from the computer or smartphone wirelessly.

One more topic I want to share here is website navigation. Many websites require the latest Flash player and be cookies enabled. What is Flash Player? It is a software by Adobe used to stream online audio, video, and rich multimedia. What are cookies? In technology terms, cookies are small amount of data saved by a web server that is distributed to web browsers. In other words, cookies are trackers of what the user does when navigating the internet.

I do not want to get too complex here. This book is about basic understanding which I hope the information provided has been basic and helpful to the reader.

Example of Conducting a Remote/WebCam Notarization

During this example, I will use DocVerify which is a platform that allows electronic signings in a secured environment that prevents fraud and protects IP. (IP stands for Internet Protocol). Each computer and smartphone has a unique IP address. The IP address is the device identifier in the internet. It is the IP that allows the device to send and receive data over the internet.

Here is the example:
(There is an appointment already set with the client. By now, the notary already has a Digital Seal, Digital Certificate, knows how to retrieve it in order to digitally sign and stamp, and knows how to use all the electronic equipment and software involved in the remote notarization).

The notary receives documents in the e-mail.
The notary uploads the documents to DocVerify.
The notary opens the electronic journal and enters the information.
The moment of the appointment arrives and the signer receives an
    e-mail from DocVerify and the steps to follow.
The client's identity is verified by a third party.
Both the notary and the client meet live in real time via Web Camera.
The remote notarization begins.

TM

Chapter 9: Review

-Hardware is the tangible parts of the computer and smartphone.

-is the intangible elements included in the computer package.

-Programs installed such as Adobe Acrobat, Microsoft Office, etc, are also considered software.

-In a smartphone, the software is recognized as the apps already installed or the downloaded ones by the mobile users.

-The signal is intangible but it is a signal not a software.

-Audio is intangible, but it is not a software, it is just audio.

-Waiting to learn how to use a computer and efficiently handle a smartphone could impact the required layers of security needed during online notarial acts.

-As basic understanding of handling electronic documents, Adobe Products are a great resource.

-Most new computers and smartphones already are wi-fi and bluetooth compatible.

-Flash Player is a software by Adobe used to stream online audio, video, and rich multimedia.

-Cookies are small amount of data saved by a web server that is distributed to web browsers.

References

https://abclegaldocs.com/blog-Colorado-Notary/notaries-in-ancient-egypt/

http://www.informednotariesofmaine.org/about-us/history

https://www.commonwealth.virginia.gov/media/governorvirginiagov/secretary-of-th
    e-commonwealth/pdf/2016-july-1-2016-handbook-update.pdf

https://www.nass.org

https://www.identrust.com

Experience.

About the Author

Hello, I am Jeannie Eunice Franks, the author of this book. I hope you have enjoyed it as much as I did writing it.

Recalling some information was very helpful to me as well. As a commissioned Notary Public, it is recommended that I often review the information I have already digested from courses, readings, and experience. Plus, one never stops learning. Here is a short version of me and why I wrote this book.

I have been serving in the United States Air Force for almost a decade. The notion of safety and security has just become embedded into my thinking and the way I operate in my daily life. I am also a trained hospital chaplain, educated in Divinity at a Master level, as well as a creative mind with a Bachelor in Fine Arts in video and digital media. For my final thesis as undergraduate, I presented a show exhibited at the Frost Museum which portrayed immersive technologies. Back in 2001, the Olympus Eye-Trek goggles were a big deal to me, so I incorporated them in my art installation as a way to give people the opportunity to experience immersion within. After graduation, I had the fortune to be hired by a broadcasting company who needed a cultural researcher. Graduating from an University where international students attended added much to my understanding , respect , and positive impact that a diverse community has over society . Reading people of all backgrounds and cultures became a natural thing to me . As a clinically trained spiritual adviser , compassion and politeness enhanced my professional ethics as well.

Traveling and participating as the Director's Assistant in an Animation and VFX International festival opened up more doors and interest in understanding how digital networks works in the cyberspace and how pixels and dots per inches are part of the same family but operate differently.

The moment I experienced my first Remote notarial act as a client, I knew I wanted to be part of that world. The technology, level of care, and the details that a Remote Notary Public has to take into consideration perfectly fit into what I already had a feel for.

Remote/WebCam Notarizations is truly a basic understanding of what online notarial acts entails. I wrote it as a warm up for notaries who will continue to polish their notarial craft.

I hope this book sparks the cyber-curiosity and cyber-safety of people who are already commissioned as Notary Public or are about to enter the notarial field in our current times when technology has the capability to enhance the notarial process without overthrowing the traditional ways needed during each and every notarial act.

Curious note about the author:

Although I am a Panther by Alma Mater connection, and have survived the Lion's Nest, at heart, I am a Hummingbird.

Self Evaluation

Why do I want to become a Notary Public?

Do I have the financial resources to become a Traditional and Electronic Notary Public? If I do not, what I am doing about it to get the resources I need to be able to afford the Commission?

Have I read the Notary Handbook of my State or Commonwealth completely?

What are the items in the Handbook I need to go over again or ask questions about?

Am I familiar with the hardware and software of the electronic devices I am planning to use during notarial acts?

Do I have all the necessary electronic devices needed during Remote/WebCam notarizations? If not, what electronic devices I need to invest in?

Am I taking great care of my health? If not, what do I need to do in order to improve my health and maintain it?

Am I taking good care of my mind, body, spirit, and social life?

What Notary Association (s) I want to join?

What Notary courses are available online and in-classroom?

What is a Digital Certificate?

What is a Digital Seal?

What is a Certifying Authority?

What are the most common notarial acts?

What is my Secretary of State's Website?

Do I know or have contact with public notaries who speak other languages?

Where do I see myself in five years?

What is a Remote/WebCam/Online Notary Public?

What is an Electronic Notary Public?

What is a Traditional Notary Public?

What is a Mobile Notary Public?

What websites sale accessories for Notaries Public?

What is a Digital Platform?

What companies offer online notarization?

What is an Error & Omission insurance?

What is a bond?

Why is the Notary Public role important?

Who grants the Notary Public Commission?

Can a Notary Public give legal advice?

What cities and counties am I willing to be available for notarial services?

If as Remote Notary I am conducting notarial services from Richmond County and my client is located in Hampton City, which location should I input in my electronic journal or/and Notary Logbook?

What is "Real Time"?

What is an eClosing?

What is the difference between an Oath and an Affirmation?

What is Cyberspace?

Why do Notaries Public have to implement extra measurements of care during Online notarizations?

What numbers related to my Notary business should I keep on my phone?

I am Commissioned Notary Public, but not a lawyer. Am I allowed by my State's Law to give legal advice?

How far am I willing to drive as a mobile eNotary?

When I am conducting Remote notarizations away from home, what are recommended items to take with me and why?

What type of computer and cellphone do I have?

What internet speed is recommended when conducting notarizations online?

How does a Digital Certificate look like? Draw it if you want to.

How does a Digital Seal look like? Draw it if you want to.

What is the name of this book?

What other books has the author of this book written?

What is the name of the author of this book?

How to contact the author if I had questions or comments about this book?

WORDS THAT ARE NEW TO ME:

If you are already a Commissioned Traditional Notary Public, practice placing your stamps and self-inked certificates below:

Notary Seal:

Acknowledgment:

Jurat:

Copy Certification:

My Notes:

◇

◇

◇

◇

◇

◇

◇

◇

◇

◇

◇

◇

◇

◇

◇

◇

◇

◇

◇

◇

◇

◇

◇

◇

◇

◇

◇

◇

◇

◇

◇

◇

◇

◇

◇

◇

◇

◇

◇

◇

◇

◇

◇

Other Notes:

If needing a logo, go here:

https://jeanniefranks1.wixsite.com/dlogosnow

https://www.facebook.com/dLogosNow **(Like and share).**

Join me on Facebook:

https://www.facebook.com/MyVirginiaNotary

Subscribe to my eNewsletter:

https://www.virginianotary.club

LARGE PRINT (bigger fonts) Notary LogBooks available at:

http://www.lulu.com/spotlight/NotaryPublic

My HashTags:

#MyVirginiaNotary
#MyVirginiaNSA
#RemoteWebCam
#RemoteWebCamNotarization

Jeannie Eunice Franks

Jeannie Eunice Franks

www.ingramcontent.com/pod-product-compliance
Lightning Source LLC
Chambersburg PA
CBHW071229170526

45165CB00003B/1043